CW00923677

The IT Infrastructure Library

IT Service Management

Version 2.1.b

Written by:	Ivor Macfarlane Colin Rudd
Edited by:	Derek Cambray
Published by:	*it*SMF Ltd Webbs Court 8 Holmes Road Earley Reading RG6 7BH United Kingdom Tel: +44 (0)118 926 0888 Fax: +44 (0)870 706 1531 e-mail: publications@itsmf.com

This version first published March 2001
Minor updates published May 2002, October 2002 and May 2003

Based on other copyright material with the permission of the copyright owners. The *it*SMF would like to thank the contributors to an extensive international quality review process for their comments.

ISBN 0-9524706-1-6

About This Guide

This pocket guide has been designed as a handy reference book for Information Technology (IT) Service Management practitioners and for those taking the Foundation Certificate in IT Service Management. It is a complementary publication to the complete IT Infrastructure Library (ITIL), which is discussed in more detail in the section on IT Service Management Best Practice.

The guide explains the processes involved in the two key areas of Service Management, and their application to the complete service life-cycle:

- Service Support
- Service Delivery

The advice contained within the guide is neither definitive nor prescriptive, but is a set of guidelines based on ITIL best practice. It is of benefit and is applicable to all IT organisations irrespective of size or the technology in use. The guidelines should be adapted and adopted to fit each organisation individually, based on the organisations':

- Business
- Culture
- Structure
- Environment
- Processes

The IT Service Management pocket guide begins with, and reinforces, the key message that IT services are there solely to support the business and its efficient and effective operation.

Contents

1 The Philosophy of Service Management

The three key objectives of Service Management are:

- To align IT services with the current and future needs of the business and its Customers
- To improve the quality of the IT services delivered
- To reduce the long-term cost of service provision.

IT has been widely utilised for decades but more recently the Internet has demonstrated that for many modern e-business based organisations:

"**IT** is the business"
and
"The business is **IT**"

It is essential therefore to recognise the absolute dependence of most businesses upon the Information and Communications Technology (ICT) infrastructure and the quantity, quality and the availability of the information that such an infrastructure provides and supports.

The challenges facing the IT Managers of today are to co-ordinate and work in partnership with the business to create new business opportunities. This has to be achieved while reducing the Total Cost of Ownership (TCO). The main method of realising this goal is the reduction of the overall management and support costs, while developing new business models to maintain or improve the quality of service delivered to the business. In order to do this the correct business and IT processes need to be developed and implemented. The management of IT is all about the efficient and effective use of the three P's: people, processes and products (tools and technology).

The ITIL philosophy adopts a process driven approach which is scaleable to fit both large and small IT organisations. It considers Service Management to consist of a number of closely related and highly integrated processes. To realise the key objectives of Service Management these processes must use the people and the products effectively, efficiently and economically in the delivery of high quality, innovative IT services aligned to business processes.

2 IT Service Management Best Practice

Best practice in IT Service Management has evolved since 1989, which saw the publication of the first elements of the IT Infrastructure Library (ITIL) by the UK Government's Central Computer and Telecommunications Agency (CCTA), (now the Office of Government Commerce (OGC)).

Available best practice now comprises integrated guidance from OGC and the British Standards Institution (BSI). Its use is supported by a qualification and training structure that has been adopted world-wide to recognise professional competence in IT Service Management.

The written guidance ranges from detailed advice on each process within ITIL, through the DISC-PD0005 Code of Practice to the formal BS15000 standard, specifying required practices for organisations.

The following diagram illustrates the need for generic guidance, such as that from ITIL and BSI. This guidance should be supported by an organisation's own internal processes and procedures.

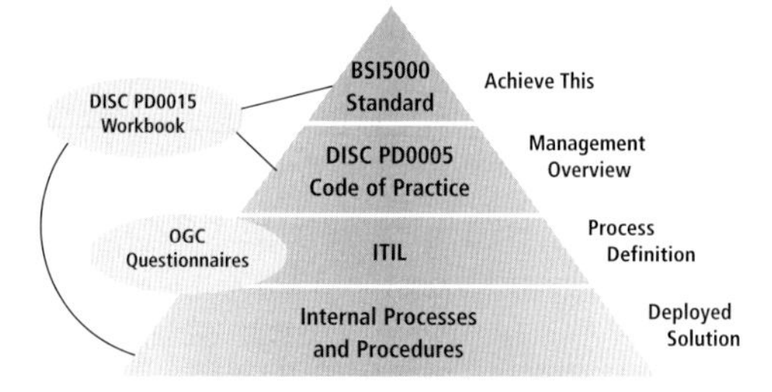

Figure 1: Guidance and Standards

ITIL Service Management

Service Management processes are at the heart of ITIL and are considered as two core areas:

Service Support	Service Delivery
*Service Desk**	
Incident Management	Service Level Management
Problem Management	Financial Management for IT Services
Configuration Management	Capacity Management
Change Management	IT Service Continuity Management
Release Management	Availability Management

** Note that Service Desk is a function not a process.*

Service Support generally concentrates on the day-to-day operation and support of IT services while Service Delivery looks at the long term planning and improvement of IT service provision.

Key Definitions

Customer: recipient of a service; usually the Customer management has responsibility for the ***funding*** of the service.

Provider: the unit responsible for the ***provision*** of IT services.

Supplier: a third party responsible for ***supplying*** or supporting underpinning elements of the IT services.

User: the person ***using*** the service on a daily basis.

Publications

Within ITIL, a major re-write exercise has been undertaken in order to consolidate and bring the material up to date, eliminate duplication, and enhance navigation. The result is a series of publications within a defined framework.

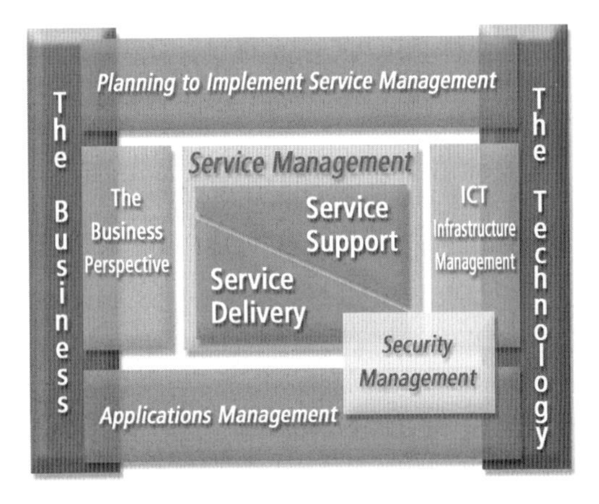

Figure 2: The ITIL Publication Framework

Best practice guidance and detailed information on the processes themselves can be found in the appropriate sections of the Service Support and Service Delivery books. This pocket guide summarises the main elements from these publications.

The complete range of ITIL and BSI publications are available from the IT Service Management Forum (*it*SMF). See Section 18 Further Information and Contact Points.

3 Implementing Service Management

Organisations should not be over ambitious when implementing Service Management. Most will already have elements established and in operation. Therefore, the Service Management implementation activity is actually one of process improvement.

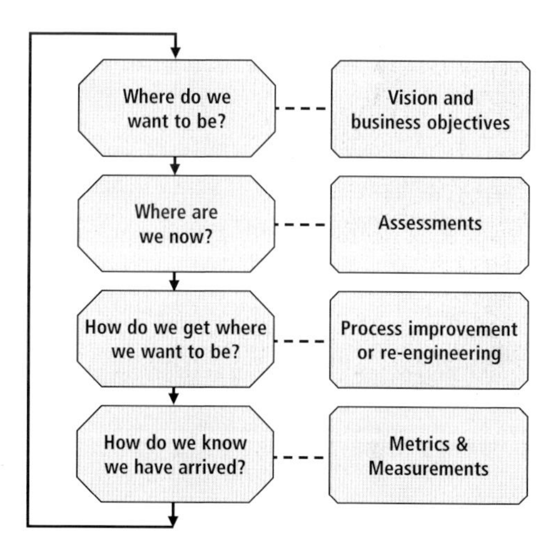

Figure 3: Process Improvement Model

Tools to assist with assessment and planning are available including self-assessment products such as BSI's workbook: PD0015.

Service Management processes can be implemented consecutively or simultaneously and each process can be broken down into a series of activities.

Overall process improvement is an iterative activity and would normally consist of the following stages:

- **Process Improvement Definition**
  - Reviewing where we are now
  - Defining the mission statement
  - Setting goals and objectives
  - Defining roles and responsibilities.
- **Communication**
  - Raising the awareness
  - Publishing and circulating information
  - Seminars, briefings and workshops.
- **Planning**
  - Producing statement of requirements
  - Designing the process improvements
  - Producing the plan
  - Identifying resources and defining the training
  - Completing a cost / benefit analysis
  - Obtaining management commitment.
- **Implementation**
  - Developing and improving the processes
  - Implementing the plan with reviews and reports
  - Developing and customising the tools
  - Training IT staff, Customers, and Users
  - Producing documentation, procedures, and deliverables
  - Testing
  - Measurement and reporting of metrics.
- **Review and Audit**
  - Review and comparison of actual achievements with goals and objectives
  - Post implementation project review
  - Identifying and publicising the benefits
  - Reviewing for effectiveness and efficiency
  - Auditing for compliance
  - Monitoring, reviewing and developing future improvements.

4 Service Support Overview

The following diagram illustrates the major interfaces and deliverables within the Service Support processes:

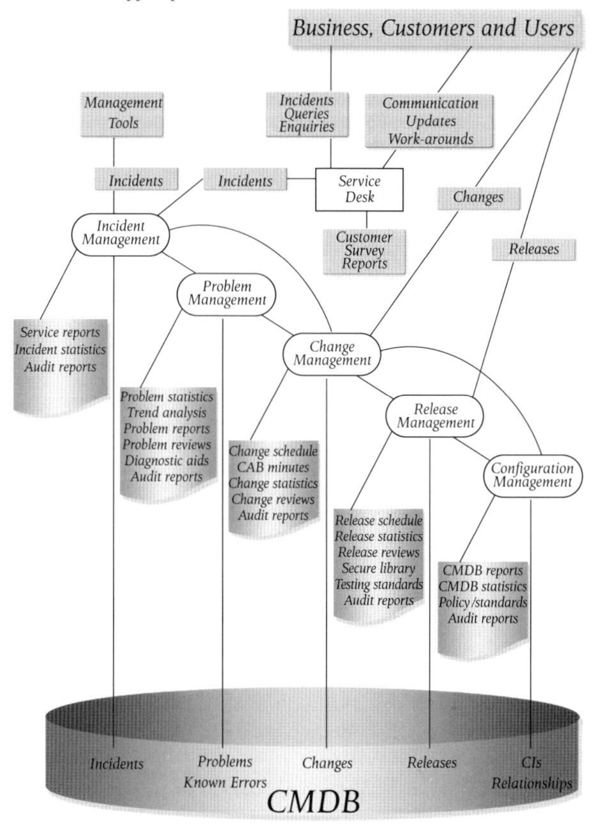

Figure 4: The Service Support Processes

5 Service Desk

Goal

To act as the central point of contact between the User and IT Service Management. To handle Incidents and requests, and provide an interface for other activities such as Change, Problem, Configuration, Release, Service Level, and IT Service Continuity Management.

Why a Service Desk?

The Service Desk, unlike other disciplines (processes) described in this book, is a function essential to effective Service Management. More than just a Help Desk, it is the principal operational interface between IT and their Users. A good first impression by each of its Users is predicated upon its performance and attitude. Often a stressful place for staff to work, underestimating its importance, high profile, and the skills required to perform the duties well, can severely hinder an organisation's ability to deliver quality IT services.

The change of name from Help Desk to Service Desk demonstrates the broader role of front line support - with more organisations looking to radically increase the percentage of calls closed at first point of contact.

The principal reasons for an organisation to invest in a Service Desk are:

- To provide a single point of contact for Users
- To deliver the high quality support critical for achieving business goals
- To help identify and lower the cost of ownership for IT services as a whole
- To support Changes across business, technology and process boundaries
- To aid User retention and satisfaction
- To assist identification of business opportunities.

Responsibilities

Most of the activities carried out by the Service Desk fall under the responsibility of one of the IT Service Management processes. The role and responsibilities of the Service Desk will depend upon the arrangements that the organisation has put in place. Among the tasks commonly assigned to the Service Desk are:

- Receive and record all calls from Users; deal directly with simple requests and complaints
- Provide initial assessment of all Incidents; make first attempt at Incident resolution and/or refer to 2nd line support, based on agreed service levels
- Monitor and escalate all Incidents according to agreed service levels
- Keep Users informed on status and progress
- Produce management reports.

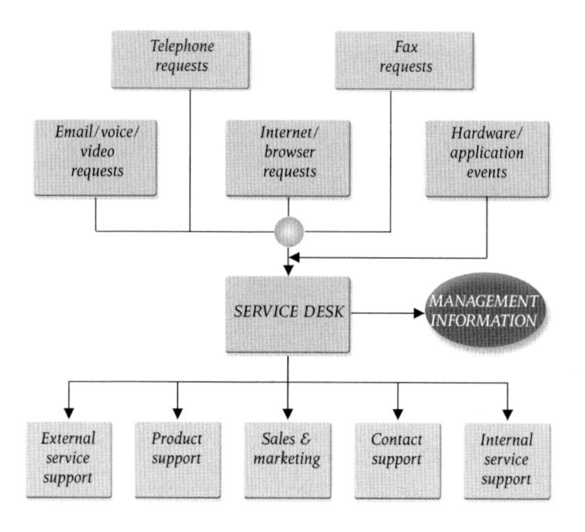

Figure 5: Incident Registration Inputs

Key Considerations

User Interaction

Expanding reporting and communication methods beyond telephone contact, such as Internet and Intranet, email and fax, can enhance service. The Service Desk still provides the main communication between the User and the IT services and:

- Represents the service provider to the User
- Considers User satisfaction and perception as critical
- Depends on the right mix of people, processes, and technology to deliver a business service.

Setting up a Service Desk

A correct Service Desk infrastructure is critical to success, and requires clear ownership, defined business goals, responsibilities, deliverables, and management commitment. The following actions need to be carried out when setting up a Service Desk:

- Ensure the business need is identified and understood
- Obtain management support, budget and resources
- Ensure the solution aligns with the service strategy
- Identify, achieve and communicate quick wins
- Define clear objectives and deliverables
- Start simply and phase the implementation
- Involve and educate Users
- Advertise and 'sell' the benefits to all parties
- Train IT staff to be Service staff.

Service Desk Technologies

A number of technologies are available to assist the Service Desk. However, remember that technology should be used to complement and enhance the service, not replace it. The technology must support correct business processes, adapting to both current and future demands. It is also important to understand that automation requires an increased need for discipline and accountability.

Types of Service Desk

Three types of Service Desk structure should be considered in establishing the optimum set-up:

- Local Service Desk
- Central Service desk
- Virtual Service Desk.

Benefits

- Improved User service, perception and satisfaction
- Increased User accessibility via the single point of contact
- Improved quality and faster response to User requests
- Improved teamwork and communication
- Better managed infrastructure and control
- More effective and efficient use of support resources
- Better management information for better decision support.

Possible Problems

- User service not considered a priority
- Lack of management commitment
- Resistance to changed working practices
- Incorrect or insufficient resources and skill levels
- Insufficient or inadequate marketing of Service Desk
- Over reliance on technology
- Insufficient funding and budget allocation.

6 Incident Management

Goal

To restore normal service operation as quickly as possible with minimum disruption to the business, thus ensuring that the best achievable levels of availability and service are maintained.

Why Incident Management?

- To ensure the best use of resources to support the business
- To develop and maintain meaningful records relating to Incidents
- To devise and apply a consistent approach to all Incidents reported.

> **Incident Definition**
>
> An Incident is any event which is not part of the standard operation of a service and which causes, or may cause, an interruption to, or a reduction in the quality of that service.

Examples of Incidents are:

- *Application* unavailable or in error
- *Hardware* outage or constrained use
- *Service Requests* for information or assistance (e.g. a service extension).

Responsibilities

- Incident detection and recording
- Classification of all Incidents, and initial support
- Investigation and diagnosis
- Resolution and recovery
- Incident closure
- Incident ownership, monitoring, tracking and communication.

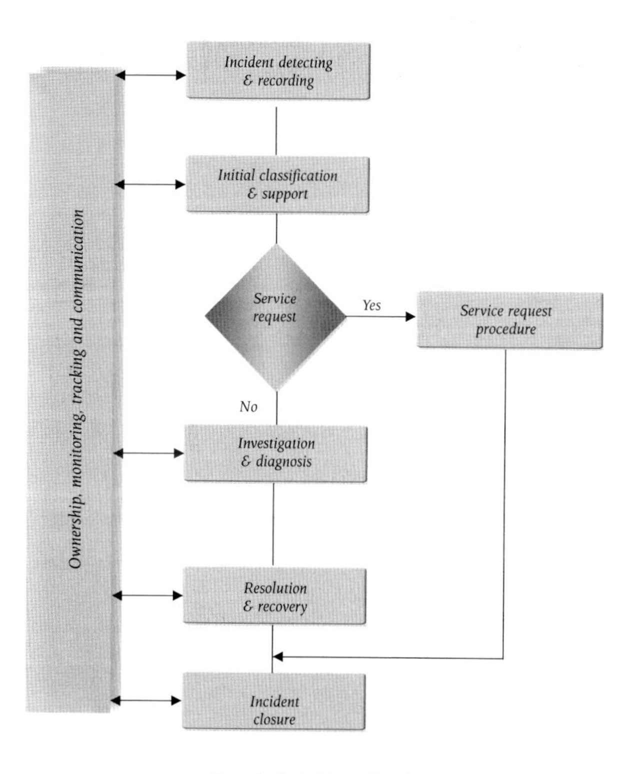

Figure 6: The Incident Life-cycle

Role of the Service Desk in Incident Management

The Service Desk will usually play the key role in the Incident Management process, recording and monitoring the progress of Incidents and retaining ownership of them.

Key Considerations

Critical Success Factors for Incident Management

- An up-to-date Configuration Management database (CMDB)
- A 'knowledge base' recording Problems and Known Error data, resolutions and workarounds
- Availability of effective automated support tools
- Close links with effective Service Level Management.

Prioritisation

Urgency is an assessment of the speed with which an Incident needs resolution.

Impact reflects the likely effect the Incident will have upon the business service.

The ***Priority*** for allocating resources to resolution of an Incident is based upon a combination of impact and urgency, together with other relevant factors such as availability of resources.

Relationship between Incidents, Problems and Known Errors

Where the cause of an Incident is not identifiable then, if investigation is warranted a Problem record is raised. A Problem represents an unknown error in one or more Configuration Items. Once the underlying cause and a workaround or correction via a Request for Change (RFC) is identified it then becomes a Known Error record. Details of relationships between Incidents, Problems, Known Errors and RFCs are held within a CMDB.

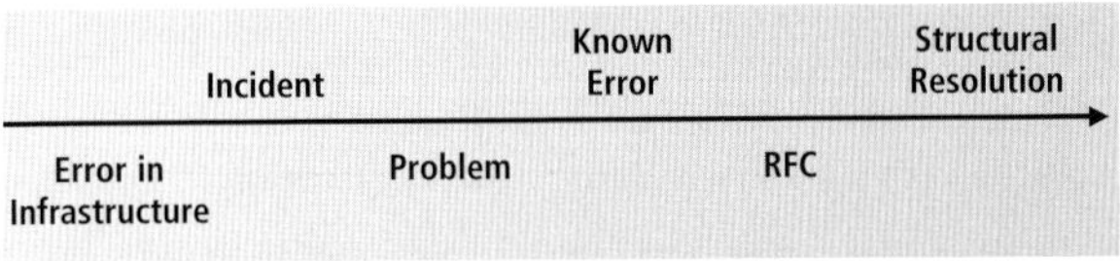

Figure 7: Logical Flow from Error to Resolution

Newly recorded Incidents will be matched against the database of existing Incidents, Problems, and Known Errors. Available workarounds will be applied to enable speedy resolution of Incidents. This knowledge base needs to be maintained so that only relevant records are presented to the Service Desk.

Handling of Major Incidents

Major Incidents occur when there is an extreme impact on the User community, or where the disruption is excessive. Problem Management must be notified and should arrange a formal meeting of people who might help. The Service Desk should ensure that a record of actions and decisions is maintained in the Incident Record.

Benefits

- Reduced business impact of Incidents by timely resolution
- Proactive identification of beneficial enhancements
- Availability of business focused information related to the Service Level Agreement (SLA)
- Improved monitoring of performance against SLAs
- Better staff utilisation leading to greater efficiency
- Elimination of lost Incidents and Service Requests
- More accurate CMDB information enabling an ongoing audit while registering Incidents
- Improved User satisfaction
- Less disruption to both IT support staff and Users.

Possible Problems

- Lack of management commitment
- Lack of agreed Customer service levels
- Lack of knowledge or resources for resolving Incidents
- Poorly integrated or missing related processes or functions
- Lack, unsuitability, or high cost, of software tools
- Users and IT staff bypassing the process.

7 Problem Management

Goal

To minimise the adverse effect on the business of Incidents and Problems caused by errors in the infrastructure, and to proactively prevent the occurrence of Incidents, Problems, and errors.

Why Problem Management?

- To resolve Problems quickly and effectively
- To ensure resources are prioritised to resolve Problems in the most appropriate order based on business need
- To proactively identify and resolve Problems and Known Errors thus minimising Incident occurrences
- To improve the productivity of support staff
- To provide relevant management information.

Problems and Known Errors

A Problem is the unknown underlying cause of one or more Incidents. It will become a Known Error when the root cause is known and a temporary workaround or a permanent alternative has been identified.

Responsibilities

- Problem control
  - Problem identification and recording
  - Problem classification
  - Problem investigation and diagnosis.
- Error control
  - Error identification and recording
  - Error assessment
  - Recording error resolution
  - Error closure
  - Monitoring resolution progress

- Assistance with the handling of major Incidents
- Proactive prevention of Problems
  - Trend analysis
  - Targeting support action
  - Providing information to the organisation
- Obtaining management information from Problem data
- Completing major Problem reviews.

Problem Control v. Error Control

Problem control focuses on transforming Problems into Known Errors. Error control focuses on resolving Known Errors via the Change Management process.

Key Considerations

Errors from the Development Environment

Errors in software released into the live environment should be incorporated into the Known Error database for live services.

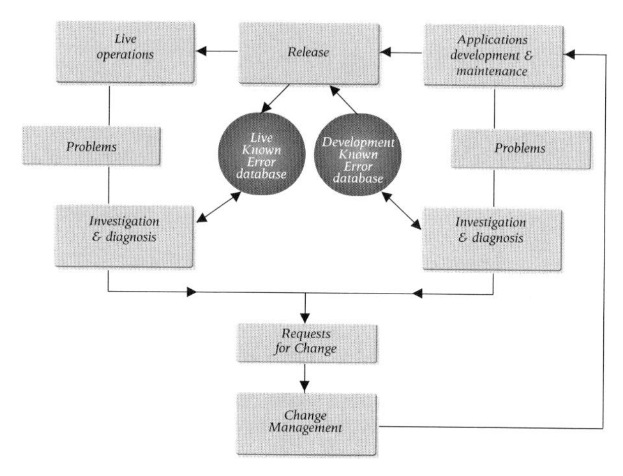

Figure 8: Errors in the Live and Development Life-cycles

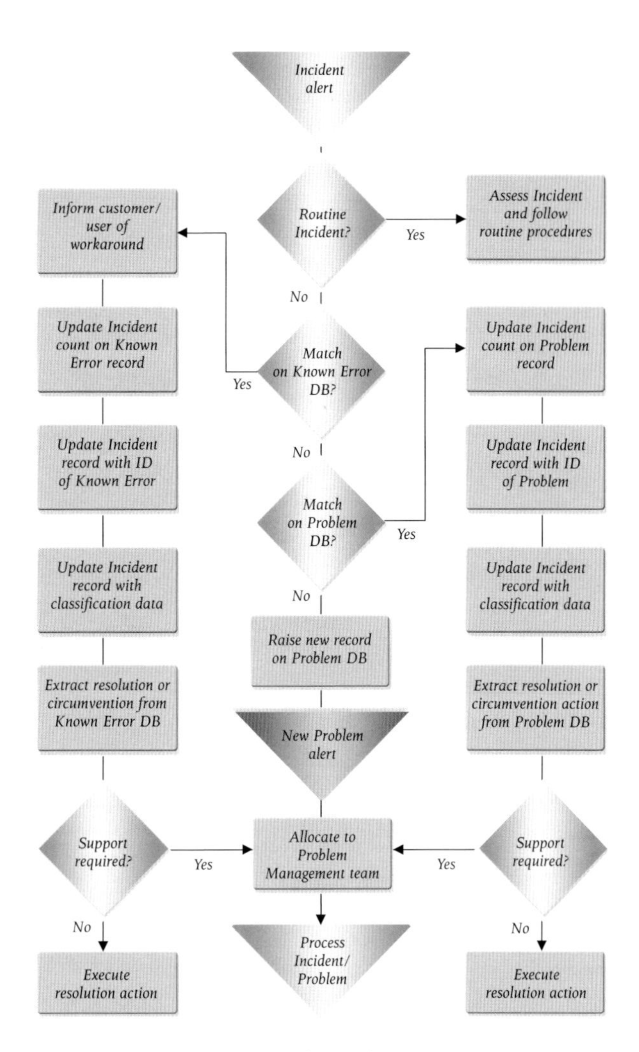

Figure 9: IT Incident Matching Process

Incident and Problem Management differences

The Incident and Problem Management processes have different imperatives. Incident Management is concerned with restoring the service to the business User as quickly as possible. Problem Management is concerned with establishing the underlying causes of an Incident, and their subsequent resolution and prevention. These goals can sometimes result in conflicting priorities.

Timing and Planning

- Good Problem Management relies on an efficient Incident Management process, so implement in parallel or immediately after Incident Management
- If resources are scarce concentrate on Problem and Error Control (reactive), and leave proactive Problem Management until later, after service monitoring activities are in place and base data is captured
- Focus on a few key Problems that are causing the greatest pain to the business - experience shows that 20% of Problems cause 80% of service degradation!

Benefits

- Improved IT services
- Incident volume reduction
- Permanent solutions
- Improved organisational learning
- Improved Service Desk first-time fix rate.

Possible Problems

- Absence of good Incident control process
- Lack of management commitment
- Undermining of the Service Desk role
- Insufficient time and resources to build and maintain the knowledge base
- Inability to accurately assess business impact of Incidents and Problems.

8 Configuration Management

Goal

To provide a logical model of the IT infrastructure by identifying, controlling, maintaining and verifying the versions of all Configuration Items in existence.

Why Configuration Management?

- To account for all IT assets
- To provide accurate information to support other Service Management processes
- To provide a sound basis for Incident, Problem, Change and Release Management
- To verify records against infrastructure and to correct exceptions.

Responsibilities

There are five basic activities of Configuration Management.

Planning

The Configuration Management plan should cover the next three to six months in detail and the following twelve months in outline. It should be reviewed at least twice a year and will include:

- Strategy, policy, scope, objectives, roles and responsibilities
- Configuration Management processes, activities, and procedures
- CMDB, relationships with other processes and third parties
- Tools and other resource requirements.

Identification

The selection, identification, and labelling of all Configuration Items (CIs). It covers recording information about CIs, including ownership, relationships, versions, and identifiers. CIs should be recorded at a level of detail justified by the business need - typically to the level of "independent change".

Control

Assurance that only authorised and identifiable CIs are accepted and recorded from receipt to disposal. It ensures that no CI is added, modified, replaced, or removed without appropriate controlling documentation, e.g. approved RFC, updated specification. All CIs will be under Change Management control.

Status Accounting

The reporting of all current and historical data concerned with each CI throughout its life-cycle. It enables changes to CIs and tracking of their records through various statuses, e.g. ordered, received, under test, live, under repair, withdrawn, or for disposal.

Verification and Audit

A series of reviews and audits that verifies the physical existence of CIs, and checks that they are correctly recorded in the CMDB. It includes the process of verifying Release and Configuration documentation before changes are made to the live environment.

Level of Control

- Identifying critical services and their components is a sensible starting point for Configuration Management
- Although low-level detail may be required in part of the structure, it may not be needed throughout
- Reviewing data levels and Configuration (CMDB) clean-up exercises can help
- Target maximum control with minimum records.

Key Considerations

Configuration Management Database

All detail and relationship information about CIs should be held in a single place, the Configuration Management Database (CMDB). This single repository of information will be accessed across the Service Management processes and is a major driver of consistency between the processes.

Relationships to other Processes

Configuration Management is closely linked with the overall Service Support and Service Delivery processes, both supporting and depending upon those processes. If those other processes are not already in existence they should be planned alongside Configuration Management.

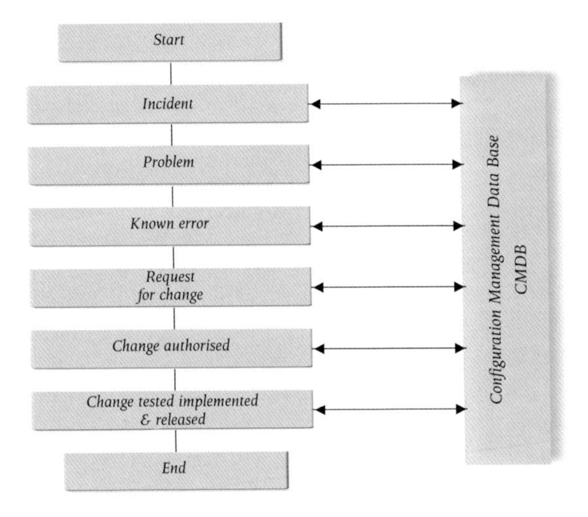

Figure 10: CMDB Interfaces to Service Support Processes

Configuration Baseline

A baseline is the configuration of a product or system established at a specific point in time, and capturing both structure and details. It can be created as a:

- Sound basis for future work
- Record of CIs affected and actually changed by an RFC
- A point to fall back to if (or when) things go wrong.

Definitive Software Library (DSL)

The Definitive Software Library is where the authorised versions of all software CIs are stored and protected. It will comprise a single logical (but probably, physically multiple) filestore for developed software and a secure physical store holding bought-in software.
(See also Release Management.)

Relationship to Asset Management

Configuration Management is not synonymous with Asset Management, which maintains details on assets, usually above a set value. Configuration Management maintains not only relevant information on the assets themselves but also information about relationships between assets.

> **Setting up Configuration Management**
>
> The planning process for setting up an appropriate function could take up to 6 months from inception to first phase of implementation. Actual implementation may take much longer, but the benefits of Configuration Management should outweigh the costs.

Benefits

- Provides accurate information on CIs and their documentation to support all other IT Service Management processes
- Facilitates adherence to legal and contractual obligations
- Helps with financial planning through clear identification of all assets and associations between them
- Makes software changes visible and supports and improves Release Management
- Improves security by controlling the versions of CIs in use, and enables the organisation to reduce the use of unauthorised software
- Facilitates impact and trend analysis for Changes and Problems.

Possible Problems

- CIs defined at too high or too low a level
- Implementation without sufficient analysis and design of the process, database and procedures, or without sufficient project planning
- Schedules or expectations that are over-ambitious
- Lack of management commitment
- Support tool lacks the required flexibility
- Process is circumvented, perceived as bureaucratic and/or is error prone
- Implemented in isolation, without necessary support from Change and Release processes
- Scope too wide or too narrow
- Not linked into application or project life-cycle.

9 Change Management

Goal

To ensure that standardised methods and procedures are used for efficient and prompt handling of all Changes, in order to minimise the impact of any related Incidents upon service.

Why Change Management?

Changes within the IT infrastructure may arise reactively in response to Problems or externally imposed requirements, e.g. legislative changes, or proactively from seeking improved efficiency and effectiveness or to enable or reflect business initiatives, or from programmes, projects, or service improvement initiatives. Change Management can:

- Ensure standardised methods, processes and procedures are used for all Changes
- Facilitate efficient and prompt handling of all Changes
- Maintain the proper balance between the need for Change and the potential detrimental impact of Changes.

Responsibilities

Change Management is responsible for controlling Change to all CIs within the live environment. It is not responsible for change within ongoing projects, which are controlled by the project change process. However close liaison between development project managers and the Change Manager is expected. Change Management would typically comprise:

- Raising and recording Changes
- Assessing the impact, cost, benefit, and risk of proposed Changes
- Developing business justification and obtaining approval
- Managing and co-ordinating Change implementation
- Monitoring and reporting on the implementation
- Reviewing and closing Requests for Change (RFCs).

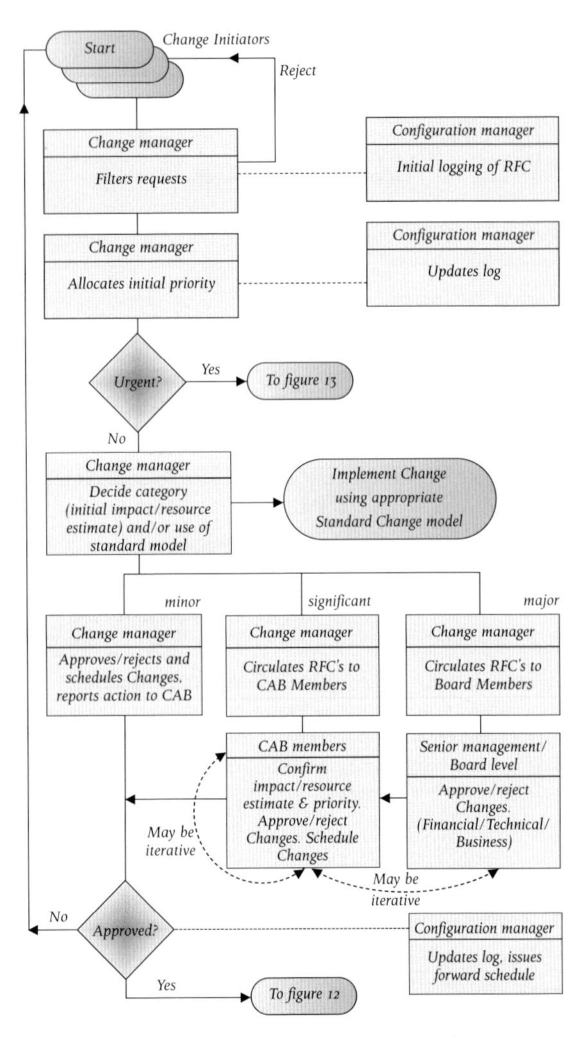

Figure 11: Change Procedures - Part 1 (normal)

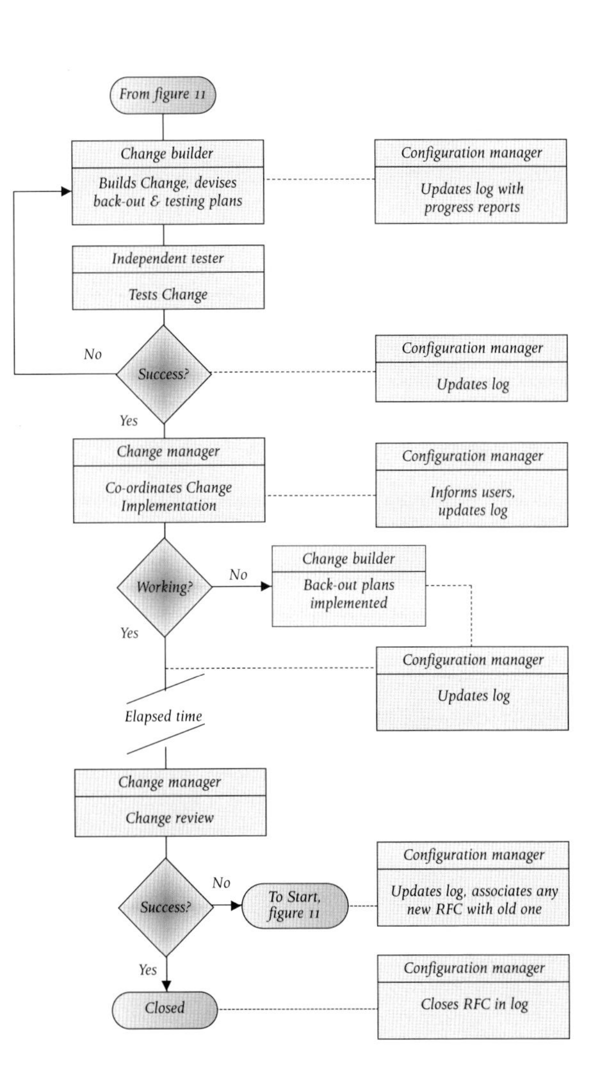

Figure 12: Change Procedures - Part 2 (normal)

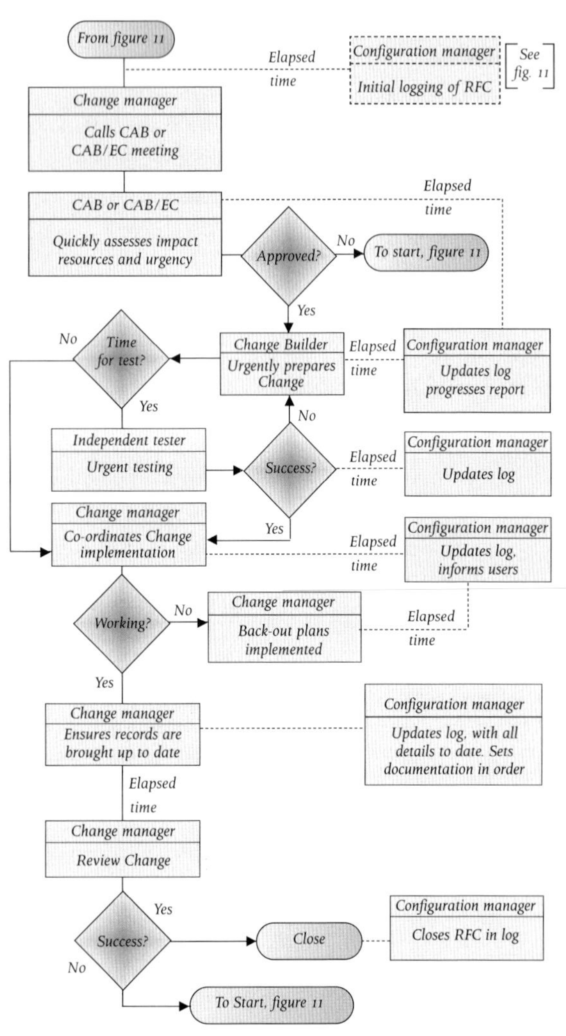

Figure 13: Change Procedures - Part 3 (urgent)

Key Considerations

Change Advisory Board

The Change Advisory Board (CAB) considers RFCs, and in the light of the business need makes recommendations as to whether they should be accepted and implemented, or rejected. Recommendations are based upon the impact on existing services, the cost of the Change, and other relevant factors. The CAB members are chosen to ensure all Changes can be adequately assessed from both the business and technical viewpoint. The CAB members are likely to include (dependent upon the agenda):

- Change Manager, chairing the process
- Relevant IT services staff
- Suppliers, maintainers and developers
- Customers and Users
- Office services and other non-IT supporting services
- Experts/technical consultants.

Face to face meetings are not always used; some CAB work takes place using electronic communications. However occasional regular meetings, e.g. twice yearly, can help to maintain the good working relationships upon which effective Change assessment depends.

When urgent major problems arise there may not be time to convene the full CAB. For these cases a CAB/EC (Emergency Committee) should be identified with authority to make emergency decisions. Membership of the CAB/EC may vary depending upon the different criteria relating to particular problems.

Change Procedures

The preceeding flowcharts illustrate the normal and urgent Change processes. Where the business impact justifies it a Change should proceed via the urgent path indicated in the flowcharts. This allows for 'fast tracking' of the process with respect to approval channels, testing, and documentation. Urgent Change procedures must not be viewed as an optional route to faster implementation since they carry considerably greater risks than normal Change procedures. The urgent procedure is typically used for emergency Problem resolution.

Standard Changes

A standard change is an accepted solution to an identifiable and relatively common set of requirements, where authority is effectively given in advance of implementation, e.g. setting up access profiles for a new employee.

Change Models

Modern tools permit the use of sophisticated Change models that can and should be used to ensure the consistent implementation of common types of changes, both major and minor, e.g. upgrade of a standard desktop software product.

> **Integration with Project Management**
>
> Change Management should be integrated with the management of large organisational programs or projects, through planning, building, testing and implementation.

Benefits

- Better alignment of IT services to the actual business need
- Increased visibility and communication of changes to both business and service support staff
- Reduced adverse impact of change on the IT service from improved business and technical impact and risk assessment
- Better assessment of the cost of proposed Changes before they are incurred
- Improved Problem, Supplier, and Availability Management through the use of valuable management information relating to Changes
- Improved productivity of Users through less disruption and higher quality services
- Improved productivity of key IT personnel, due to less distraction to repair faulty Changes
- Greater ability to absorb a large volume of Changes.

Possible Problems

- Scope incorrectly set, e.g. over-stretching staff, Changes not aligned to project life-cycle, or inability to address all aspects of Change
- Lack of ownership and knowledge of impacted systems making impact assessment impossible
- Staff resistance to a process perceived as too bureaucratic
- Lack of visible management commitment and support to enforce the process
- Lack of control over urgent Changes
- Lack of an accurate CMDB.

10 Release Management

Goal

To take an holistic view of a Change to an IT service and ensure that all aspects of a Release, both technical and non-technical, are considered together.

Why Release Management

Release Management should be used for:

- Large or critical hardware roll-outs
- Major software roll-outs
- Bundling or batching related sets of Changes.

Release Management co-ordinates the many service providers and suppliers involved with a significant Release of hardware, software and associated documentation across a distributed environment.

Responsibilities

- Planning and overseeing the successful roll-out of new and changed software and associated hardware and documentation
- Liaison with Change Management to agree the exact content and roll-out plan for the Release
- Ensuring that all items being rolled out or changed are secure and traceable via the CMDB
- Managing Customers and Users expectations of Releases and roll-outs.

Release Policy

A Release policy document should be produced to clarify the roles and responsibilities for Release Management. There may be one document per organisation, or an umbrella set of guidelines and specific details for each supported system or IT service.

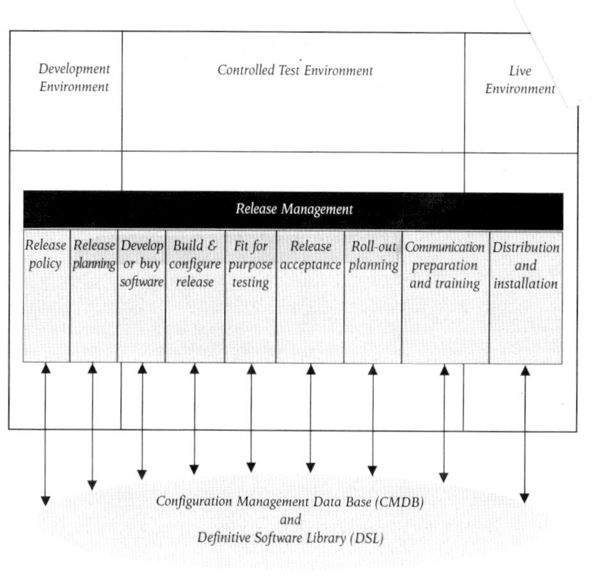

Figure 14: Major Activities of Release Management

Key Considerations

Types of Release

Full Release: all components of the Release are built, tested, distributed and implemented together.

Delta Release: only those CIs that have actually changed since the last Release are included.

Package Release: individual Releases, both full and delta, are grouped together to form a package for Release.

Definitive Software Library (DSL)

The DSL contains the master copies of all controlled software in an organisation, including purchased software as well as software developed on-site. The exact configuration of the DSL that is required for Release Management should be defined before development commences.

The following should be considered:

- Media
- Naming conventions
- Environments supported
- Security arrangements
- Scope
- Retention period
- Audit procedures.

The CMDB should be updated and referred to throughout the Release Management process, concurrently with updates to the DSL.

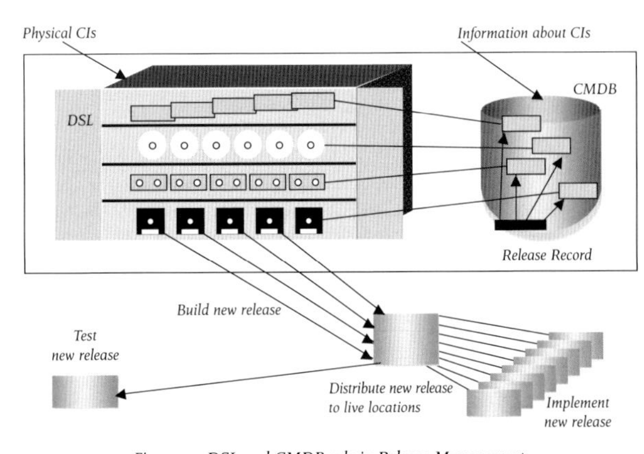

Figure 15: DSL and CMDB role in Release Management

Definitive Hardware Store (DHS)

An area should be set aside for the secure storage of definitive hardware spares. Spares should be maintained at the same level as the live location, and their details recorded in the CMDB.

Build Management

The software and/or hardware components that comprise a new Release should be assembled in a controlled manner to ensure a reproducible process. It is quite common to automate the build process to reduce the reliance on human intervention and so make it more reliable. Build management becomes the responsibility of Release Management from the controlled test environment onwards.

Testing and Back-out Plans

Releases should undergo stringent testing and User acceptance before release. Back-out plans, to document the consequent action should a Release fail, wholly or partly, must exist. The back-out plans should be tested as a part of the overall Release testing process.

Change, Configuration, and Release Management

A central function for Change, Configuration and Release Management offers considerable advantages. Without Change Management, Configuration information will rapidly become inaccurate, without accurate Configuration data, Change impacts are not accurately assessable, and without Configuration and Change Management, Releases will not be controllable.
A recommended approach is to have a single Change and Configuration Management and Release Plan that addresses:

- Combined roles and responsibilities
- Nature of the CMDB, DSL, and DHS together with associated tool and library requirements
- Change, Configuration and Release Management procedures as they relate to each other.

Definitions

Release: a collection of authorised Changes to an IT Service.

Release Unit: the portion of the IT infrastructure that is normally released together.

Roll-out: deliver, install and commission an integrated set of new or changed CIs across logical or physical parts of an organisation.

Benefits

When combined with Configuration Management, Change Management and operational testing, Release Management can deliver:

- Improved service quality as a result of a greater success rate for Releases and minimisation of disruption to the business
- Assurance that hardware and software in live use is of known quality, reducing the chance of illegal, wrong, or unauthorised software being in use
- Better use of resources, either User, testing, or development
- Greater ability of the organisation to cope with high levels of Change
- Better expectation setting for business and service support staff.

Possible Problems

- Resistance from staff to new procedures
- Circumvention or inappropriate use of 'urgent' procedures
- Unclear ownership and role acceptance between operational and development staff
- Inadequate building and testing of Releases, due to insufficient hardware resources
- Inability to recreate all possible environments
- Lack of understanding of the full contents of a Release or pressure to roll-out before a Release is fully prepared
- Reluctance to back-out a failing Release.

11 Service Delivery Overview

The following diagram illustrates the major interfaces and deliverables within the Service Delivery processes:

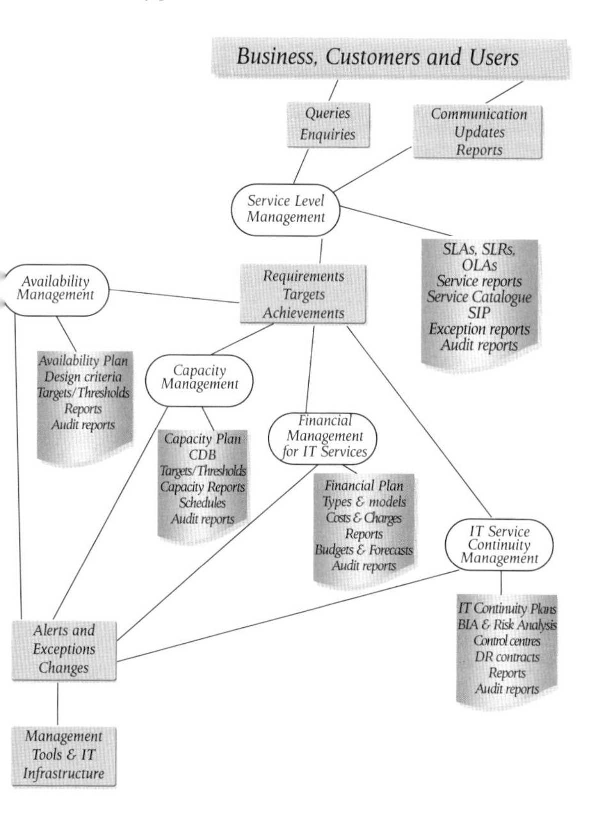

Figure 16: The Service Delivery Processes

12 Service Level Management

Goal

To maintain and gradually improve business aligned IT service quality, through a constant cycle of agreeing, monitoring, reporting and reviewing IT service achievements and through instigating actions to eradicate unacceptable levels of service.

Why Service Level Management?

Service Level Management (SLM) ensures that the service targets are documented and agreed in Service Level Agreements (SLAs) and monitors and reviews the actual service levels achieved against their SLA targets. SLM should also be trying to proactively improve all service levels within the imposed cost constraints.

Service Level Management is the process that manages and improves agreed levels of service between two parties:

- The provider, who may be an internal service department (e.g., engineering, computer department, building services), or an external outsourcing company or third party supplier
- The receiver of the service, i.e. the Customer who pays the bills.

Responsibilities

- Negotiating and agreeing service requirements and expected service characteristics with the Customer
- Measuring and reporting of:
  - Service Levels actually being achieved against target
  - Resources required
  - Cost of service provision
- Continuously improving service levels in line with business processes, with a Service Improvement Programme (SIP)
- Co-ordinating other Service Management and support functions, including third party suppliers

- Reviewing SLAs to meet changed business needs or resolving major service issues
- Producing, reviewing and maintaining the Service Catalogue.

Service Catalogue

Service Level Management will document the services provided to the Customers, detailing the key features of those services, preferably within the CMDB. This catalogue will form the basis for an understanding of all the services offered, their components, features, charges, etc.

There may well be the need for a version of the Service Catalogue aimed at Customers, as well as one holding more supplier-related information.

Key Considerations

Customer Focus

The Service Level Management process encourages both Provider and Customer to realise that they have joint responsibility for the service. Typically this generates:

- An understanding of the Customer's business processes and drivers
- An acceptance of the benefits of early discussions of expected changes to workload volumes or the nature of the service
- Constructive discussions on better ways of meeting the Customers' needs and of transforming business processes.

The SLM Process

The SLM process creates a management framework that disciplines both the Provider and the Customer. SLM encourages the Customer to consider, document and define their real business needs. SLM generally makes the Provider more focused and accountable. By including the cost of the IT services in the measurements, the SLM processes can also help improve the cost effectiveness of the services.

Content of Service Level Agreements

As a minimum, a Service Level Agreement should include:

- A simple description of the service and the deliverables
- The agreed service hours
- User response times, Incident response times and resolution times, and response times to Changes
- Service availability, security and continuity targets
- Customer and Provider responsibilities
- Critical business periods and exceptions, (holidays, escalation, etc.).

All targets contained within an SLA should be capable of being monitored and measured.

When the service is being provided to an external Customer the SLA will normally supplement a contract that will define the minimum acceptable level of service.

Structure of Service Level Agreements

Some organisations have chosen to adopt a multiple level SLA structure. One example of a three-layer structure might be as follows:

- Corporate Level: covering all the generic SLM issues appropriate to every Customer throughout the organisation (such as response times when calling the Service Desk)
- Customer Level: covering all SLM issues relevant to the particular Customer group, regardless of the service being used.
- Service Level: covering all SLM issues relevant to the specific service, in relation to a specific Customer group (1 for each service covered by the SLA).

Operational Level Agreements (OLAs)

OLAs are also known as 'back-to-back' agreements. They define support requirements internally. The most common use of an OLA is to define the relationship between the Service Desk and internal support groups.

OLAs are required to ensure that the SLA targets agreed between Customer and Provider can be delivered in practice. OLAs describe each of the separate components of the overall service delivered to the Customer, often with one OLA for each support group and a contract for each supplier. OLAs or SLAs may be agreed with external suppliers to supplement external contracts.

Underpinning Contracts

It is important to ensure that all targets contained within both SLAs and OLAs that rely on external suppliers, are underpinned by the appropriate level of maintenance and support contracts, and are documented and agreed within such contracts.

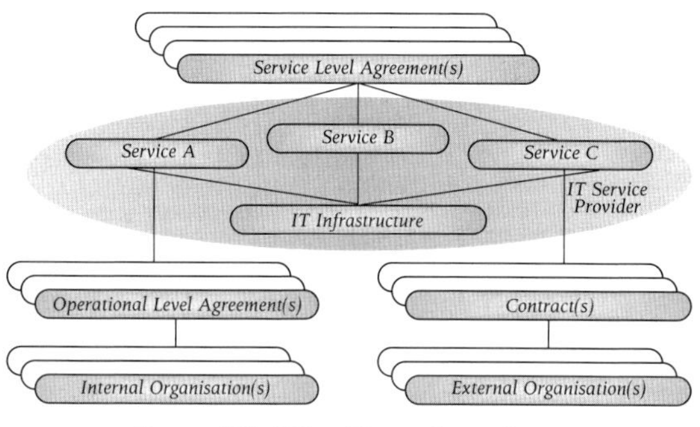

Figure 17: SLA, OLA and Contract Support Structure

Service Improvement Programme

SLAs generally concentrate on the quality of service that will be delivered in the next twelve months. In rapidly changing environments a Service Improvement Programme (SIP) should be produced to demonstrate to the Customers the steps that will be taken to improve the service in the next revision of the SLA.

> **Beyond SLAs**
>
> Many organisations consider SLM to consist purely of the creation of SLAs that are then promptly forgotten about. In reality a SLA is a means to an end, a mechanism for the management of a relationship, between Customer and Provider, for mutual benefit.
>
> The true benefits of Service Level Management will come only when both parties see the benefits of their active involvement in the whole process.

Benefits

- Both parties have a clearer view of responsibilities and there are specific service targets to aim for
- Service monitoring and reviews will allow weak areas to be identified, so that remedial action can be taken
- Misunderstandings between Customers and IT Service Providers are avoided
- SLM underpins supplier management and SLAs are a key part of managing supplier relationships
- IT services will be designed to meet Service Level Requirements (SLRs) of future business requirements
- SLAs can be used as a basis for charging and will demonstrate what Customers receive for their money
- OLAs and support contracts with external suppliers are better aligned with the business services required.

Possible Problems

- Ensuring targets are verified and achievable before agreeing and committing to them
- Monitoring, measuring, and reporting of actual achievements
- Incorrect scoping, with inadequate resources and time
- Not enough seniority/authority given to SLM to push through negotiations/improvements
- SLAs may not be supported by adequate underpinning contracts or agreements
- SLAs may be too lengthy, not concise, not business focused and therefore not used
- Business requirements not clearly understood with no business justification for the requested service levels
- Lack of focus on business critical services/processes
- A resistance to change
- The service levels to be provided are dictated to Customers
- Customer perception and expectation
- SLM not used to trigger service improvements
- SLM not aligned with the complete service life-cycle.

13 Financial Management for IT Services

Goal

To provide cost effective stewardship of the IT assets and the financial resources used in providing IT services.

Why Financial Management for IT Services?

Financial Management for IT Services is an integral part of Service Management. It provides the essential management information to ensure that services are run efficiently, economically, and cost effectively. An effective financial management system will:

- Assist in the management and reduction of overall long term costs
- Identify the actual cost of services and their provision
- Provide accurate and vital financial information to assist in decision making
- Identify how IT adds value to the Customer's business
- Enable the calculation of Total Cost of Ownership and Return on Investment
- Make Customers aware of what services actually cost, if appropriate
- Support the recovery of costs, from Customers if appropriate, in a fair and equitable manner
- Provide measurements of Value For Money, and provide incentives to produce quality services aligned to business needs
- Help influence Customer behaviour, for example by providing incentives for using non-critical resources
- Encourage more efficient use of resources
- Provide better cost information and control of external contracts and suppliers
- Assist in the assessment and management of Changes.

Responsibilities

- Enable the organisation to account fully for the spend on IT services and to attribute these costs to the services delivered to the organisation's Customers
- Assist management decisions on IT investment by supporting detailed business cases for Changes to IT services
- Control and manage the overall IT budget and enable the fair and equitable recovery of costs (by charging) for the provision of IT services.

Key Considerations

Concepts

Budgeting and Accounting (mandatory): understanding the cost of providing each service, whether recovered or not, is essential to the delivery and maintenance of cost effective and efficient services. These activities enable an organisation to:

- Predict the money required to run IT services for a given period
- Ensure that the actual spend can be compared with the predicted spend at any point
- Account for the money spent in IT services in a given period
- Calculate the cost of IT service provision.

Charging (optional): can have clear business benefits, acting as an incentive to the Provider and giving leverage to the Customer who can demand Value for Money. Charging enables an organisation to:

- Recover the cost of the IT services from the Customers of the service
- Operate the IT Services as a business unit if required.

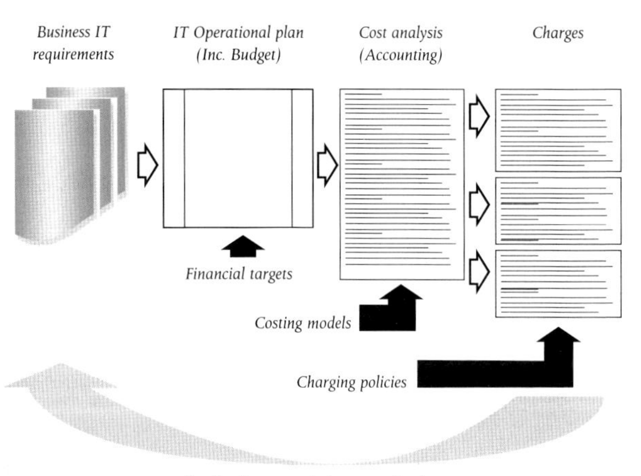

Figure 18: Costing, Charging and Budgeting Cycle

Charging

Charging needs to be seen as being simple, understandable, fair and realistic. Senior IT and Business Managers will set the charging policy. Possible charging policies are:

Cost:	price = cost
Cost-plus:	price = cost ± X%
Going rate:	price is comparable with other internal departments' costs within the organisation or with similar organisations
Market rate:	price matches that charged by external suppliers
Fixed price:	a set price is agreed for a set period with the Customer based on anticipated usage

Cost Elements

Typical major cost types for an organisation's costs might be:

Type	Includes
Hardware	Mainframes, disk storage, networks, PCs, portables, local servers
Software	Operating systems, applications, databases, monitoring and management tools
People	Payroll costs, benefits, re-location costs, expenses, consultancy
Accommodation	Offices, storage, secure areas, utilities
External Service	Security services, Disaster Recovery services, outsourcing services
Transfer	Internal charges from other cost centres within the organisation

Each cost can be categorised for accounting purposes between different alternatives, including the following:

Either	Or
Capital Outright purchase of fixed assets e.g. new server	**Operational** Day-to-day costs of running a service: staff, electricity, maintenance, consumables
Direct Costs which can be directly allocated to a single Customer or Customer group	**Indirect** Costs which must be apportioned across all or a number of Customer groups
Fixed Costs fixed for a reasonable period of time (salaries, depreciation, standing charges)	**Variable** Costs that vary with usage or time (overtime, electricity etc.)

Cost Model

A framework, in which all known costs necessary to calculate the overall costs of IT service provision can be recorded and allocated to specific Customers. Most Cost Models are based on calculating the cost for each Customer but other models can be developed to show the cost for each service or the costs for each location.

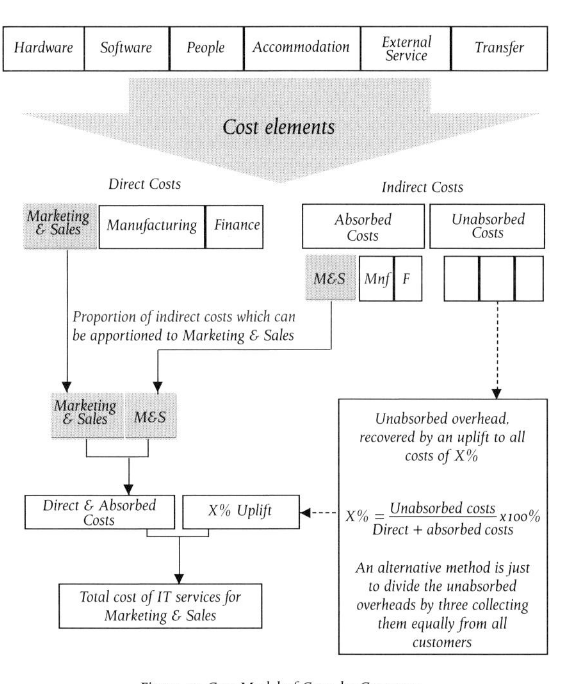

Figure 19: Cost Model of Costs by Customer

Benefits

- Reduced long term costs
- Increased confidence in setting and managing budgets
- Accurate cost information to support IT investment
- More efficient use of IT throughout the business
- Increased awareness and professionalism within IT
- Ensuring that the business provides sufficient funds to run the IT services it requires
- More business-like decision making on IT services
- Recovering IT costs in a fair manner, related to usage
- Influencing Customer and User behaviour
- Allowing comparison with alternative service Providers.

Possible Problems

- Budgeting, accounting and charging are often new disciplines in IT and there are limited skills available
- The lack of availability of planning information both within and outside IT, could cause problems and delays
- IT staff with accountancy skills are rare, so key activities may rely on uncommitted external resources
- Enterprise IS strategies and objectives may not be well developed and prediction of capacity not accurate
- Senior IT and Business Managers may resent the administrative overheads of financial processes
- IT may not be able to respond to changes in Customer demands once costs become an influence
- The financial processes are so elaborate that the cost of the system exceeds the value of the information
- The monitoring tools providing resource usage information are inaccurate, irrelevant or too costly
- If charges are seen as excessive Customers may go elsewhere for their IT services.

14 Capacity Management

Goal

To understand the future business requirements (the required service delivery), the organisation's operation (the current service delivery), the IT infrastructure (the means of service delivery), and ensure that all current and future capacity and performance aspects of the business requirements are provided cost effectively.

Why Capacity Management?

Capacity Management ensures that IT processing and storage capacity provision match the evolving demands of the business in a cost effective and timely manner. The process encompasses:

- Monitoring the performance and the throughput of IT services and supporting IT components
- Tuning activities to make efficient use of resources
- Understanding the current demands for IT resources and deriving forecasts for future requirements
- Influencing the demand for resource, in conjunction with other Service Management processes
- Producing a Capacity Plan predicting the IT resources needed to achieve agreed service levels.

Success in Capacity Management

Success depends on a number of factors:

- Accurate business forecasts
- An understanding of current and future technologies
- An ability to demonstrate cost effectiveness
- Interaction with other effective Service Management processes
- An ability to plan and implement the appropriate IT capacity to match business need.

INPUTS	SUB-PROCESSES	OUTPUTS
• *Technology* • *SLAS, SLRS and Service Catalogue* • *Business Plans and Strategy* • *IS, IT Plans and Strategy* • *Business requirements and volumes* • *Operational schedules* • *Deployment and Development plans and programmes* • *Forward schedule of Change* • *Incidents and Problems* • *Service reviews* • *SLA breaches* • *Financial plans* • *Budgets*	*Business Capacity Management:* • *Trend, forecast, model, prototype, size and document future business requirements* *Service Capacity Management:* • *Monitor, analyse, tune and report on service performance, establish baselines and profiles of use of services, manage demand for service.* *Resource Capacity Management:* • *Monitor, analyse, tune and report on the utilisation of components, establish baselines and profiles of use of components*	• *Capacity Plan* • *Capacity Database* • *Baselines and profiles* • *Thresholds and alarms* • *Capacity reports (regular ad hoc and exception)* • *SLA and SLR recommendations* • *Costing and charging recommendations* • *Proactive changes and service improvement* • *Revised operational schedule* • *Effectiveness reviews* • *Audit reports*

Figure 20: The Capacity Management Process

Responsibilities

There are three principal areas of responsibility:

Business Capacity Management (BCM):

Is responsible for ensuring that the future business requirements for IT services are considered, planned and implemented in a timely fashion. These future requirements will come from business plans outlining new services, improvements and growth in existing services, development plans etc. This requires knowledge of:

- Existing service levels and SLAs
- Future service levels and SLRs
- The Business Plan and Capacity Plan
- Modelling techniques (Analytical, Simulation, Trending, and Baselining)
- Application sizing methods.

Service Capacity Management (SCM):

Focuses on managing the performance of the IT services provided to the Customers, and is responsible for monitoring and measuring services, as detailed in SLAs and collecting, recording, analysing and reporting on data. This requires knowledge of:

- Service levels and SLAs
- Systems, networks, and service throughput and performance
- Monitoring, measurement, analysis, tuning and demand management.

Resource Capacity Management (RCM):

Focuses on management of the components of the IT infrastructure and ensuring that all finite resources within the IT infrastructure are monitored and measured, and collected data is recorded, analysed and reported. This requires knowledge of:

- The current technology and its utilisation
- Future or alternative technologies
- The resilience of systems and services.

Key Considerations

Overlapping Activities

The Service and Resource Capacity Management sub-processes carry out many similar activities. However the two sub-processes each have a very different focus: the former is focused on the services that support the business, and the latter is focused on the technology that underpins all the service provision.

Performance and Capacity Issues

Capacity Management should be the focal point for all IT performance and capacity issues. Other technical domains, e.g. network management, may carry out the bulk of the relevant day-to-day duties, but overall responsibility should lie with a centralised Capacity Management process.

Iterative Activities

The main Capacity Management activities of monitoring, analysis, tuning, and implementation, are iterative in nature.

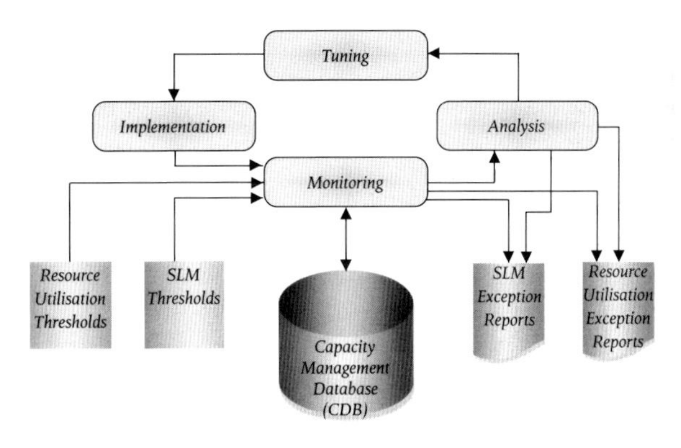

Figure 21: Iterative Capacity Management Activities

The Capacity Management Database

The Capacity Management Database (CDB) is used as the basis for the production of all Capacity Management reporting on existing and future capacity issues. It is unlikely to be a single database, but will probably exist in several physical locations and will contain many different types of data, including:

- Business data
- Service data
- Technical data
- Financial data
- Utilisation data.

Capacity Management and the Business

Capacity Management must understand the technical infrastructure and its capabilities and also the likely effects of the use of new equipment and technologies.

However, even more importantly, it must also work closely with the business. It needs to be able to translate business predictions and workload estimates into capacity requirements, in terms of quantity, and determine when they will be required.

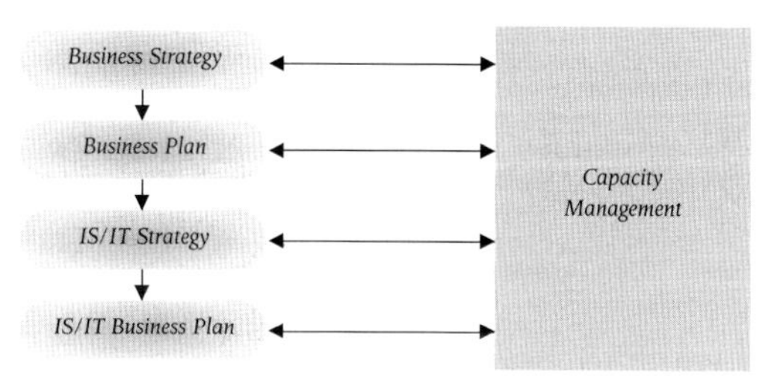

Figure 22: Capacity Management and the Business

Demand Management

This is an important aspect of the interface between the business and Capacity Management, and has the objective of influencing demand and therefore the use of resources. It requires a full understanding of the business requirements and their demands on IT services and resources. It must be carried out sensitively and without causing damage to the business, Customers, Users, or the reputation of IT.

> **A Balancing Act**
>
> Capacity Planning is essentially a balancing act:
>
> - Cost against capacity
> - Supply against demand.

Benefits

- Increased efficiency and cost savings resulting in more economic provision of IT services
- Deferred expenditure
- Elimination of unnecessary spare capacity and optimisation of equipment
- Elimination of expensive panic buying
- Reduced risk of performance Problems and failure
- More confident and improved forecasting
- Early and improved awareness of capacity issues within the application development life-cycle
- Better and more informed acquisition of IT resources
- Better relationships with Customers and Users with improved understanding of service levels and SLAs
- Service improvements through better control
- Less need for reactive support.

Possible Problems

- Customer expectations exceed technical capacity
- Over expectation of the benefits to be gained from tuning
- Unrealistic and unachievable performance figures from equipment suppliers and manufacturers
- Unavailability of necessary business information due to commercial and/or security concerns
- Unreliable and inaccurate business forecasts and information
- Incomplete or inaccurate information, particularly from distributed systems, networks and PCs
- Too much data: many tools provide vast amounts of capacity information
- Lack of financial resources, and technical resources and skills.

15 IT Service Continuity Management

Goal

To support the overall Business Continuity Management process by ensuring that the required IT technical and services facilities can be recovered within required and agreed business time-scales.

Why IT Service Continuity Management?

IT Service Continuity Management is concerned with managing an organisation's ability to continue to provide a pre-determined and agreed level of IT services to support the minimum business requirements, following an interruption to the business. This includes:

- Ensuring business survival by reducing the impact of a disaster or major failure
- Reducing the vulnerability and risk to the business by effective risk analysis and risk management
- Preventing the loss of Customer and User confidence
- Producing IT recovery plans that are integrated with and fully support the organisation's overall Business Continuity Plan.

Responsibilities

- The available IT Service Continuity options must be understood and the most appropriate solution chosen in support of the business requirements
- Roles and responsibilities need to be identified, and endorsed and communicated from a senior level to ensure respect and commitment for the process
- IT recovery plans and Business Continuity Plans should be aligned, and regularly reviewed, revised and tested.

Roles in Normal Operation	Roles in Crisis Situation
Board Level	
Initiate IT Service Continuity, set policy, allocate responsibilities, direct and authorise	Crisis management, corporate decisions, external affairs
Senior Management	
Manage IT Service Continuity, accept deliverables, communicate and maintain awareness, integrate across organisation	Co-ordination, direction and arbitration, resource authorisation
Junior Management	
Undertake IT Service Continuity analysis, define deliverables, contract for services, manage testing and assurance	Invocation, team leadership, site management, liaison and reporting
Supervisors and Staff	
Develop deliverables, negotiate services, perform testing, develop and operate processes and procedures	Task execution, team membership, liaison

Key Considerations

IT and Business Continuity Awareness

The best way to raise awareness is to highlight the potential risks and business impacts facing an organisation. Awareness of the need for IT Service Continuity Management will come from:

- The range of risks facing an organisation and its vulnerability
- The potential business impacts that could result should any of the risks materialise
- The likelihood of each of the risks materialising
- Personal responsibilities and liabilities, e.g. of directors
- External pressures, e.g. from regulators or shareholders.

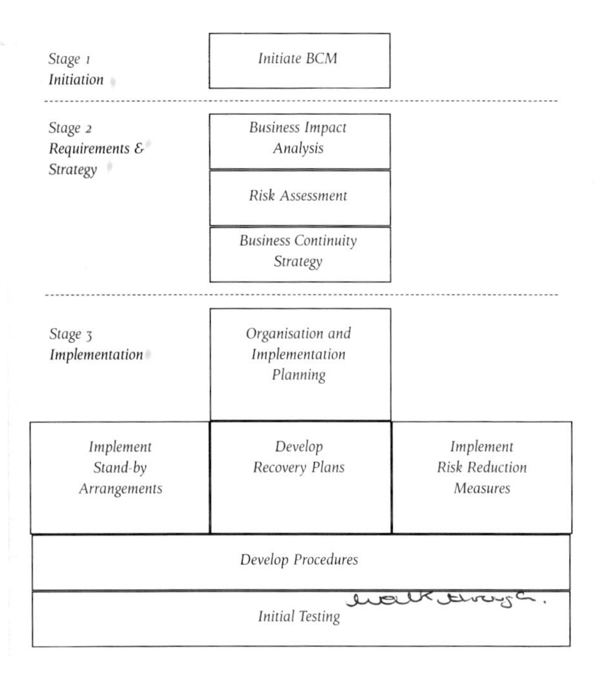

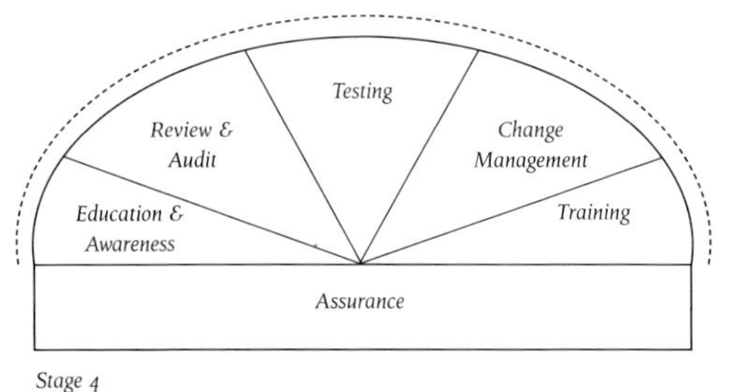

Stage 4
Operational Management

Figure 23: The Business Continuity Life-cycle

Options need to be considered for:

- People and accommodation
- IT systems, networks, and processes
- Critical services such as power, water, post, etc.
- Critical assets such as paper records, reference material, etc.

Option	Description
Do nothing:	Rarely used, because few business processes can function effectively without IT.
Manual back-up:	Can be an effective interim measure until the IT service is resumed.
Reciprocal arrangement:	Organisations agree to back each other up in an emergency, rarely used now except for off-site storage because of practical difficulties, e.g. limited excess IT capacity.
Gradual recovery: *(Sometimes referred to as "cold standby")*	Usually consists of an empty computer environment in which an organisation can install its own equipment. May be used where a business can function for a period of 72 hours or more without IT services. Can be internal or external, fixed or portable, possibly with guaranteed equipment delivery.
Intermediate recovery: *(Sometimes referred to as "warm standby")*	Typically involves the re-establishment of critical systems and services within a 24-72 hour period. Can be internal or external, fixed or portable, and consists of a computer environment containing recovery IT equipment that can be configured to support the business.
Immediate recovery: *(Sometimes referred to as "hot standby")*	Would involve the use of an alternative site with continuous mirroring of live equipment and data. Can be internal or external and is the most expensive option. Would only be used for critical business services where loss of service would cause an immediate business impact.

Risk Analysis

Many methods of risk assessment and analysis exist, such as the CCTA Risk Analysis and Management Method (CRAMM). This involves the identification of risks, the associated threats, vulnerabilities and impacts together with the subsequent implementation of cost justifiable countermeasures.

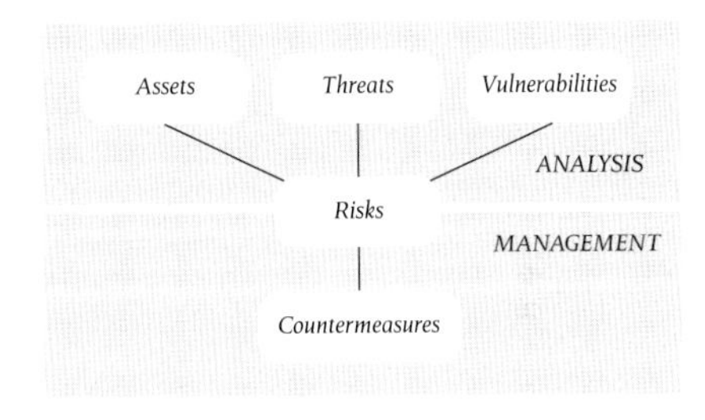

Figure 24: The CRAMM Risk Assessment Model

Benefits

- Management of risk and the consequent reduction of the impact of failure
- Potentially lower insurance premiums
- Fulfilment of mandatory or regulatory requirements
- Improved relationships between the business and IT through IT becoming more business focused, and more aware of business impacts and priorities
- Reduced business disruption during an incident, with an ability to recover services efficiently in business priority order
- Increased Customer confidence, possible competitive advantage and increased organisational credibility.

Possible Problems

- Obtaining management commitment and resources
- Gaining buy-in and assistance from the business
- The process and cost of testing and invoking plans for live services
- Availability of components, resources and data to test the IT recovery and Business Continuity Plans
- Overlooking critical components, applications, and dependencies, and misinterpreting business impacts
- Incorrect business impacts and/or business focus
- Poor integration with other business and Service Management processes.

Testing the Recovery Plan

Plans should be tested after initial development, and thereafter at least annually, and following major Changes. Testing will range from inspection or walk-through, to announced testing of components, or to full unannounced tests involving the business and IT.

16 Availability Management

Goal

To optimise the capability of the IT infrastructure and supporting organisation to deliver a cost effective and sustained level of availability that enables the business to satisfy its objectives.

Why Availability Management?

Availability Management ensures services are available when the Customer needs them, and is influenced by:

- Business demand
- The cost required to meet it
- The Configuration and complexity of the IT infrastructure including, the level of redundancy, the reliability of the infrastructure and its components, and the levels of infrastructure maintenance
- The processes and procedures used by IT services
- Human factors and external events.

Responsibilities

- Optimise availability by monitoring and reporting on all key elements of availability
- Determining availability requirements in business terms
- Predicting and designing for expected levels of availability and security
- Producing the Availability Plan
- Collecting, analysing and maintaining availability data and reporting on that data
- Ensuring service levels are met by monitoring service availability levels against SLAs, and monitoring OLA targets and external supplier serviceability achievements
- Continuously reviewing and improving availability.

Key Considerations

Elements of Availability Management

Availability: the percentage of the agreed service hours for which the component or service is available

Reliability: the prevention of failure, and the ability to keep services and components operable

Maintainability: the ability to restore services or components back to normal operation

Serviceability: the support for which external suppliers can be contracted to provide parts of the IT infrastructure

Security: the implementation of justifiable controls to ensure continued IT service within secure parameters, viz: Confidentiality, Integrity and Availability. (For more detail refer to the ITIL Security Management publication, or to BS7799/ISO17799 - The Information Security Management standards.) Security should be considered in all aspects of the following diagram:

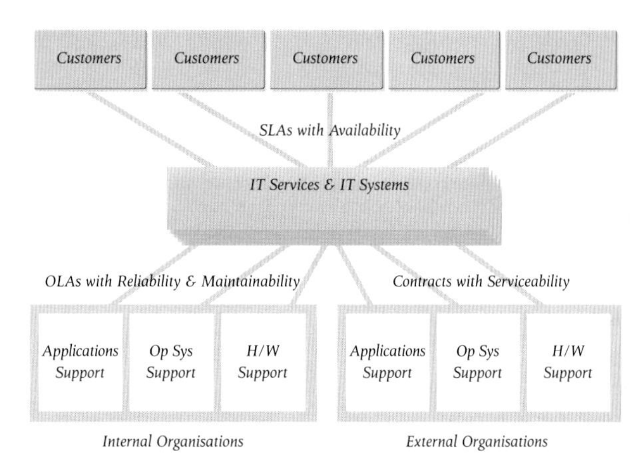

Figure 25: Relationships with Support Organisations

Availability Metrics

The IT Availability Metrics Model (ITAMM) assists in assessing the range of metrics and perspectives that should be considered when establishing availability measurement and reporting. The model can be used to establish what needs to be measured in order to give a comprehensive view of the availability of IT services.

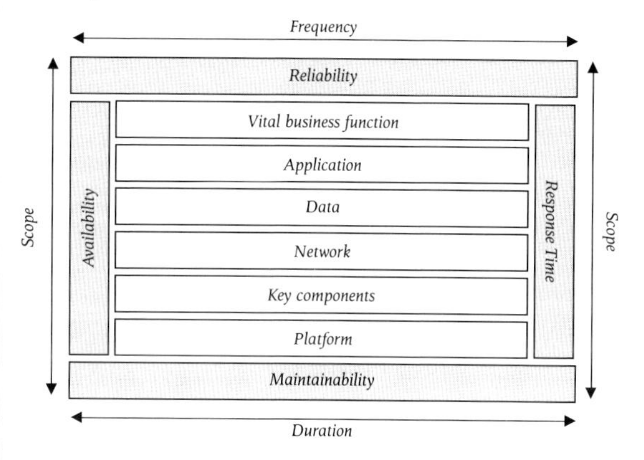

Figure 26: The IT Availability Metrics Model

> **Measuring Availability**
>
> Measurements need to be meaningful and add value if availability measurement and reporting are to ultimately deliver benefit to the IT and business organisation. This will be strongly influenced in the combination of "what you measure" and "how you report it".

The Availability Plan

The Availability Plan should be a long-term plan for the proactive improvement of IT availability within the imposed cost constraints. The plan should have goals, objectives and deliverables and should consider the wider issues of people, processes, tools and techniques as well as having a technology focus.

Availability Management Principles

- Availability is at the core of business need and User satisfaction
- Recognising that when things go wrong, you can still achieve User satisfaction
- Improving availability can only begin when you understand how the technology integrates with and supports the business.

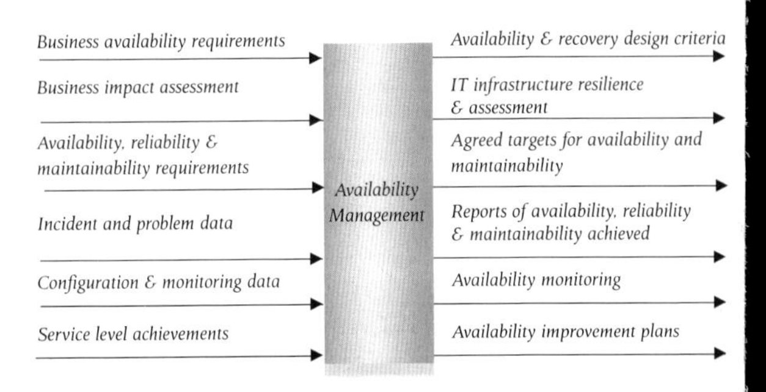

Figure 27: The Availability Management Process

Useful Definitions

High Availability:	a characteristic of the IT service that minimises or masks the effects of IT component failure to the User.
Continuous Operation:	a characteristic of the IT service that minimises or masks the effects of planned downtime to the User.
Continuous Availability:	a characteristic of the IT service that minimises or masks the effects of ALL failures and planned downtime to the User.

enefits

- Addresses the fundamental business requirement for high levels of availability
- Services are designed and managed to cost effectively meet specified business requirements
- Availability levels are measured to fully support Service Level Management
- Shortfalls in service levels are identified and corrective actions taken
- Frequency and duration of IT failures is reduced
- Change IT mindset from a reactive to a proactive attitude
- IT support "adds value" to the business.

ossible Problems

- Measures of availability that are meaningless to the business
- Not measuring availability at the point of service delivery
- Difficulties in finding skilled and experienced staff
- Justification to management in relation to expenditure
- Lack of management commitment
- Lack of suitable software
- Dependence on suppliers for serviceability data, i.e. reliability and maintainability
- Difficulty in determining business and Customer availability requirements
- Lack of information about the IT infrastructure, if there is no Configuration Management database.

Business Value

Effective Availability Management will influence Customer satisfaction and determine the perceived reliability of the business on the market.

17 The Importance of Communication

Effective and efficient communication is part of the foundation on which th success of many organisations depends. In the business world there are man pressures on time, and often it is communication that suffers when time an resource constraints apply. In Service Management there are many areas tha are involved in regular communication with their business Customers t ensure that the services delivered to them meet their requirements a appropriate cost. Notable examples include Service Desk, Chang Management, and Service Level Management.

Everyone within IT has a responsibility to provide good communication bu there is a prime responsibility at the management level to ensure tha communication is embedded within the Service Management process.

Developing and fostering effective communication with Customers and User of IT has always been an important issue. Very often this was something tha was left almost to chance and to the personal actions of individuals within I departments. In the modern business world this is not sufficient.

Organisations can be said to operate at three key levels; strategic, tactical, an operational, and there are specific corporate functions at each level. For IT to b fully integrated with their business Customers, effective two-way communicatio must take place at the same three levels and also between these levels.

The ability to listen, influence, negotiate, and agree is vital.

Many communication techniques exist, and include: seminars, report circulars, e-mail, memos, newsletters, meetings, awareness campaigns, focu groups, presentations, road-shows, Internet, and Intranet.

The Need for Improvement

During review exercises of organisational, departmental, or team performance, communication is one of the most commonly mentioned topics that people suggest requires improvement.

18 Further Guidance and Contact Points

itSMF Ltd.
Webbs Court
3 Holmes Road
Earley
Reading RG6 7BH
United Kingdom
Tel: +44(0)118 926 0888
Fax: +44 (0)870 706 1531
e-mail: service@itsmf.com
www.itsmf.com

The itSMF is a totally independent, not-for-profit organisation owned and run by its members. It promotes and helps to set the standards for best practice in IT Service Management. There are national chapters in many parts of the world. For further details of the chapters, and how to contact them, access the web site or contact the UK office.

OGC
Rosebery Court
St Andrews Business Park
Norwich NR7 0HS
United Kingdom
Tel: +44(0)845 000 4999
Fax: +44(0)1603 704 618
e-mail: servicedesk@ogc.gsi.gov.uk
www.ogc.gov.uk
www.itil.co.uk

British Standards Institution
389 Chiswick High Road
London W4 4AL
United Kingdom
Tel: +44(0)208 996 9001
Fax: +44(0)208 996 7001
e-mail: info@bsi-global.com
www.bsi-global.com